Hell

Mesopotamia

Creating and Solving Word Problems

Bonnie Coulter Leech

PowerMath™

The Rosen Publishing Group's
PowerKids Press™
New York

Published in 2007 by The Rosen Publishing Group, Inc.
29 East 21st Street, New York, NY 10010

Book Design: Daniel Hosek

Photo Credits: Cover © Stapleton Collection/Corbis; pp. 7 (top), 9 (background) © Nik Wheeler/Corbis;
pp. 7 (bottom), 28 © David Lees/Corbis; pp. 9 (jar), 15, 17, 22 © Gianni Dagli Orti/Corbis;
p. 10 © Michael S. Yamashita/Corbis; p. 13 © Bridgeman Art Library; p. 18 © Yann Arthus-Bertrand/Corbis;
p. 23 (background) © Paul Almasy/Corbis; p. 24 © Ashmolean Museum, University of Oxford, UK/Bridgeman
Art Library.

Library of Congress Cataloging-in-Publication Data

Leech, Bonnie Coulter.
  Mesopotamia : creating and solving word problems / Bonnie Coulter Leech.
      p. cm. — (Math for the real world)
  Includes index.
  ISBN 1-4042-3357-1 (library binding)
  ISBN 1-4042-6067-6 (pbk.)
  6-pack ISBN 1-4042-6068-4
  1. Word problems (Mathematics)—Juvenile literature. 2. Problem solving—Juvenile literature. I. Title. II.
Series.

  QA63.L44 2006
  510—dc22

                                    2005013543

Manufactured in the United States of America

Contents

Mesopotamia

Have you ever wondered where the earliest known human civilizations began? Historians think that the land between the Tigris and Euphrates rivers was the origin of the first permanent human settlements. This is why it is often called the "cradle of civilization." The name "Mesopotamia" comes from Greek words meaning "land between the rivers." It refers not only to the land between the Tigris and Euphrates rivers but to the surrounding area as well, from the mountains of eastern **Asia Minor** to the Persian Gulf.

Between 7000 B.C. and 5000 B.C., wandering peoples known as nomads settled along the banks of the Tigris and Euphrates rivers. This area provided abundant natural resources and fertile soil. The land between the rivers was so rich that the people quickly settled into farming. They were the first people to build plows and plant seeds. The settlers learned to control flooding and found better ways to water the farmland by creating the first **irrigation** canals. The fertile land produced crops such as barley, wheat, sesame, **flax**, and various fruits and vegetables.

The great quantity of food available made conditions suitable for civilizations to develop. In this book, we will create and solve word problems to learn more about the ancient civilizations of Mesopotamia and about their many contributions to modern civilization.

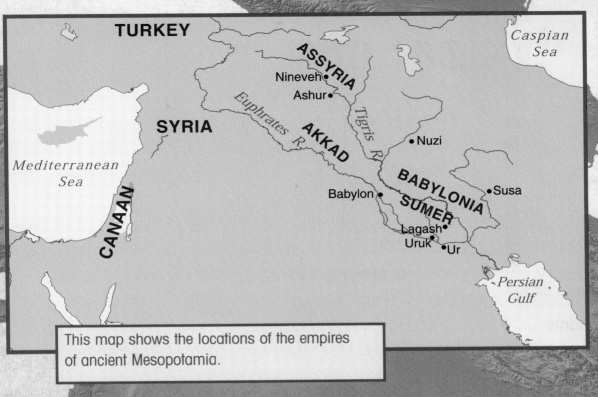

This map shows the locations of the empires of ancient Mesopotamia.

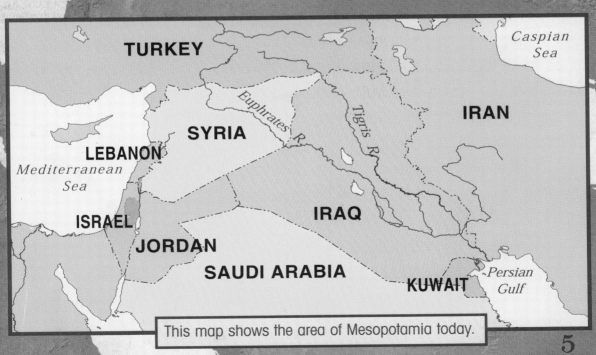

This map shows the area of Mesopotamia today.

5

Civilizations

Before civilization began, nomads traveled in small groups from place to place. While in each area, the people would eat the food that grew wild and hunt wild animals. When the food and animals were no longer plentiful, the nomads would move on.

The land between the Tigris and Euphrates rivers was different. Its rich land offered an ideal place to grow food, which allowed people to stop moving around and remain in a location. Instead of hunting, the former nomads began to **domesticate** animals. The small farming villages slowly grew into larger settlements, creating the first civilizations.

There are 4 characteristics that are present in a civilization. One is surplus food. The rivers of Mesopotamia provided the water necessary to grow crops for food. There was also an abundance of natural resources, fish, and wild animals.

Another characteristic is workers with special jobs. The surplus of food meant that not everyone had to spend their time growing food. This allowed the development of other special jobs, such as soldiers, blacksmiths, merchants, and builders.

A civilization also has a system of writing. With the increase of farming and trade, the people of Mesopotamia developed a way of keeping records and communicating.

The fourth characteristic of a civilization is social organization, which includes government and religion. These governments and religions may be set up in many ways. In early civilizations, priests served as both religious leaders and rulers.

Ur was one of the early cities that developed in the region known as Mesopotamia. Its ruins, below, can still be seen today.

nall statues like these below were placed
Sumerian temples to represent
orshippers in constant prayer to the gods.

The fertile land between the Tigris and Euphrates rivers was approximately 300 miles long and 150 miles wide. What is the area of a rectangular plot of land with the same dimensions?

To find the area of a rectangle, use the formula Area = length x width.

$$A = l \times w$$
$$A = 300 \times 150$$

$$
\begin{array}{r}
300 \\
\times\ 150 \\
\hline
000 \\
15\ 00 \\
+\ 30\ 0 \\
\hline
45{,}000 \\
\end{array}
$$

A = 45,000 square miles

The area of the rectangular plot of land is 45,000 square miles.

If you know the length and width of a piece of land, you can create and solve an area word problem like the one above. Try it.

As the small farming villages grew, they became independent city-states consisting of villages and towns with populations as large as 50,000 people. A city-state was made up of the city and the farmland that surrounded it.

The city-states were not all the same. Each had its own religion, language, ruler, and government. They operated under a **theocracy** in which a priest-king ruled as both religious leader and king. City-states tried hard to keep their independence even if conquered by another ruling power. This created a long history of battles and exchanges of power.

The important ancient civilizations in early Mesopotamia included Sumer, Akkad, Babylonia, and Assyria. Each of these early civilizations showed evidence of early forms of agriculture, writing, literature, calendars, and mathematics.

Let's say that the total number of people in 4 city-states was 85,700. What was the average number of people in each city-state?

To solve this problem, divide the total number of people by the number of city-states.

total number of people (85,700) ÷ number of city-states (4)

$$4 \overline{)85{,}700} = 21{,}425$$

There was an average of 21,425 people in each of the 4 city-states.

Can you create a word problem about the average number of people in 2 city-states? Use the above problem as a model.

Sumerian city-states like Ur and Uruk (pictured in the background) developed the plow, the potter's wheel, and bronze, which is a mixture of copper and tin.

This jar was created in Sumer around 3000 B.C. Early pots typically were decorated with geometric or animal designs painted in black or red on a light background.

Sumerians

Around 3500 B.C., the Sumerians migrated into southern Mesopotamia and began building large cities. They created a culture that would influence many civilizations. The city-states of Sumer, located in what is now Iraq, controlled areas of several hundred square miles and included the cities of Ur, Uruk, Kish, Lagash, and Eridu.

At the center of each city-state was a very large, pyramid-shaped temple built on a platform with 3 to 7 terraced levels. These temple-towers were called **ziggurats**. The ziggurat was the first major building structure of the Sumerians. It was made of sun-baked mud bricks and was colorfully decorated. The Sumerians believed that these temples connected heaven and Earth.

The Sumerians were polytheistic (pah-lee-thee-IHS-tihk), which means they worshipped many gods. Every city-state had its own god or goddess, who gave special help to its people. Many of the gods had a ziggurat dedicated to them with a shrine located at the top. Although religious events were held at the ziggurats, only the priest-kings were permitted inside them.

The Sumerian city-state of Ur contained a ziggurat, pictured here, that honored the moon-god, Nanna.

Suppose the mud bricks used to build a ziggurat were 13.25 inches long, 13.25 inches wide, and 3.25 inches high. What would be the total surface area of each brick?

13.25 in
3.25 in
13.25 in

To find the surface area, first find the area of each side of the brick.

There are 6 sides.

There are 4 sides measuring 13.25 inches by 3.25 inches. Surface area for these 4 sides is 13.25 x 3.25 x 4, or 172.25 square inches.

13.25 in
3.25 in

```
      13.25
    x  3.25
      6625
     2 650
   +39 75
    43.0625
```

```
    43.0625
    x      4
    172.2500
```

There are 2 sides measuring 13.25 inches by 13.25 inches. Surface area for these 2 sides would be 13.25 x 13.25 x 2, or 351.125 square inches.

13.25 in
13.25 in

The total surface area would be 172.25 square inches + 351.125 square inches, or 523.375 square inches.

```
      13.25
    x13.25
      6625
     2 650
    39 75
  + 132 5
   175.5625
```

```
    175.5625
    x        2
    351.1250
```

One of the elements that define a civilization is an organized government. The Sumerians had a well-developed government to oversee and govern the large areas and diverse peoples of the city-states. The early Sumerian priest-kings' duties included leading the military, overseeing trade, judging disputes, and serving as religious leaders. Under each priest-king were several officials, mostly priests, who surveyed the land, assigned fields to farmers, set tax rates, and distributed crops after the harvest.

Early in Sumerian civilization, 80% to 90% of those who farmed worked on their own land. Farming was hard work, and those who failed to harvest enough crops were forced to borrow from others. If farmers could not harvest enough crops to repay their debts, they lost their land. Sumerian priests once farmed the land alongside other farmers. However, as the government developed, the priests separated from the commoners. They became the greatest landowners among the Sumerians, and others worked the priests' land.

The Sumerian city-state of Ur grew to about 24,000 people. If 80% of the people were farmers, about how many people farmed the land?

To find out how many people farmed the land, multiply 24,000 by 80%.

First change 80% to a decimal. Eighty percent means "80 out of 100" or $\frac{80}{100}$.

$\frac{80}{100} = 0.80$

$$\begin{array}{r} 24{,}000 \\ \times \quad .8 \\ \hline 19{,}200.0 \end{array}$$

About 19,200 people in Ur were farmers.

This Sumerian ruler
known as Gudea ruled
the city-state of Lagash
around 2100 B.C. He
was known for bringing
peace to his land as
well as for his devotion
to the gods.

Babylonians

The Sumerians lived in an unpredictable time. Throughout the history of Mesopotamia, wars between city-states and invasions from foreign lands were common. The Sumerians were constantly at war with each other and with other peoples migrating into the region. The Akkadians, a group of people who migrated north from the Arabian Peninsula, finally conquered and unified the Sumerian city-states. Even though the Akkadians were in power, they adopted the Sumerian culture, including its government, economy, writing, law, religion, and legends. Although the Sumerian people seemed to disappear after being conquered, their **legacy** lived on for centuries.

The Akkadians had formed the world's earliest empire, Akkad, which was first ruled by Sargon I. Around 2200 B.C., the Akkadians lost control of their empire to invaders from the northeast. Independent city-states became strong again about 100 years later. Then, around 1800 B.C., southern Mesopotamia was united into a single empire by the city-state of Babylon. Its ruler Hammurabi (ham-uh-RAHB-ee) had created the kingdom of Babylonia.

If Sargon I ruled from 2334 B.C. to 2279 B.C., how many years did he rule over the Akkadian empire?

To solve this word problem, subtract 2279 from 2334. Be sure to add 1 to the answer to include the first year that Sargon ruled.

$$
\begin{array}{r}
2334 \\
- \ 2279 \\
\hline
55 \text{ years} + 1 \text{ year}
\end{array}
$$

Sargon I ruled the Akkadian empire for 56 years.

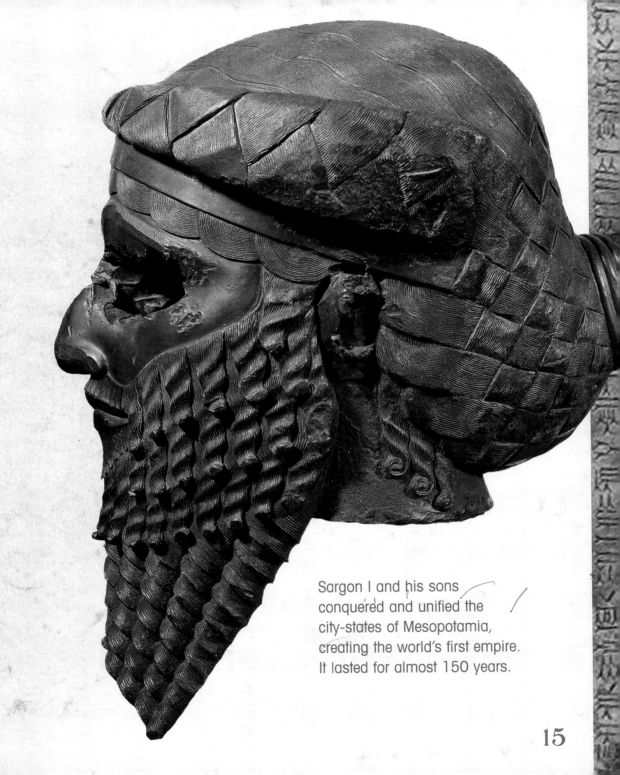

Sargon I and his sons
conquered and unified the
city-states of Mesopotamia,
creating the world's first empire.
It lasted for almost 150 years.

Hammurabi, the best known of the kings of the Old Babylonian Empire, ruled from about 1790 B.C. to 1750 B.C. He pushed the boundaries of the empire to the Mediterranean Sea, unifying most of Mesopotamia. The people of Mesopotamia saw many reforms and accomplishments during Hammurabi's rule, such as an improved irrigation system, taxation methods, and government structure. The people were united under 1 religion. The time of Hammurabi's reign is often referred to as the "Golden Age of Babylon."

Hammurabi was a successful military leader and ruler, but he is best remembered for his code of laws. The Code of Hammurabi was a set of 282 laws written in stone and placed in a public location for everyone to see. The laws required all people to be responsible for their actions. However, the laws changed often and not all people had to follow them. Punishment was often unequal for the same offense. An offense could draw a punishment of death or just a small fine, depending on the offender's place in society.

Some Laws from the Code of Hammurabi

If anyone bring an accusation of any crime before the elders, and does not prove what he has charged, he shall, if it be a capital offense charged, be put to death.

If anyone is committing a robbery and is caught, then he shall be put to death.

If anyone open his ditches to water his crop, but is careless, and water flood the field of his neighbor, then he shall pay his neighbor corn for his loss.

If a man put out the eye of another man, his eye shall be put out.

If he put out the eye of a man's slave, or break the bone of a man's slave, he shall pay one-half of its value.

If a man knock out the teeth of his equal, his teeth shall be knocked out.

This stone carving depicts Shamash, the sun god, handing the code of laws to Hammurabi. The sun god, seated on the throne, can be identified by the flames on his shoulders.

17

Around 1600 B.C., the Hittites conquered the Babylonians. The Hittites have a mysterious origin. It is believed that they invaded Babylonia from the area now known as Turkey. The Hittites adopted the laws, religion, and literature of the Babylonians as the Akkadians and Babylonians had adopted the culture and ways of the Sumerians.

The Hittite empire covered all of Mesopotamia. Since their primary activity was commerce, the Hittites traded with all civilizations and peoples of the Mediterranean. As the trade routes spread, so did Mesopotamian culture, religion, law, government, economy, and ideas. The Hittite cities remained independent until around 720 B.C., when they were conquered by the Assyrians.

Over the next several centuries, many empires of the Mesopotamian region would rise and fall. **Archaeological** discoveries of the past 150 years have shown how much the peoples of Mesopotamia have affected the modern world.

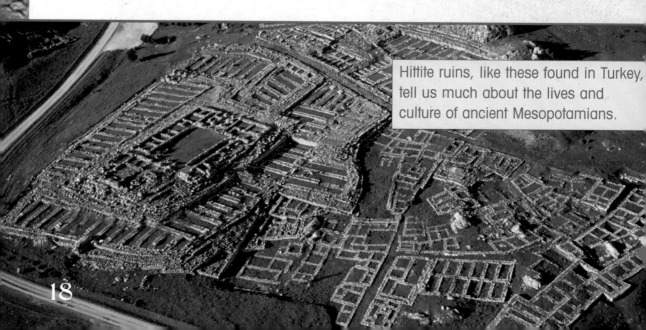

Hittite ruins, like these found in Turkey, tell us much about the lives and culture of ancient Mesopotamians.

If you were asked to create a word problem using the timeline below, what kind of problem would you create? Since a timeline often shows us the order and times of events, you could create a problem about the amount of time between 2 dates. Solve the problem below.

According to the timeline, about how many years passed between the beginning of the earliest settlements in Mesopotamia and the Assyrians conquering the Hittites?

To answer this question, subtract to find the difference between the 2 dates.

$$\begin{array}{r} 5,000 \\ -720 \\ \hline 4,280 \end{array}$$

About 4,280 years passed between the 2 events.

Can you create and solve another word problem using the timeline?

Mesopotamia Timeline

5000 B.C.
Permanent settlements
begin in northern
Mesopotamia

2300 B.C.
Akkadians
conquer
Sumerians

1600 B.C.
Hittites
conquer
Babylon

3500 B.C.
Sumerians
establish first
cities

1790 B.C.
Hammurabi
begins rule of
Old Babylonian
Empire

720 B.C.
Assyrians
conquer
Hittites

Cuneiform Writing

One of the major contributions of early Mesopotamian civilizations was the development of writing. By around 3100 B.C., the ancient Sumerians had developed writing as a means of keeping records of trade. The early writing of the Sumerians started with pictures or sketches of words they wanted to represent. They used reeds to write on wet clay. The clay tablets were then dried in the sun to become hardened tablets.

Gradually, the Sumerians improved their writing system. The development of cuneiform (kyoo-NEE-uh-form) made writing faster, easier, and more efficient. The Sumerians wrote with triangular-shaped sticks to form hundreds of different wedge-shaped markings on moist clay tablets. However, not everyone learned to read and write. Young boys around 8 years old who were believed to have been chosen by the gods were taught cuneiform. They finished their training when they were 20 years old.

Like cuneiform letters, cuneiform numbers were written using wet clay as a writing medium. The chart on page 21 shows the early Sumerian numbers from 1 to 60. Notice that these cuneiform numbers were written using a combination of 3 wedge-shaped markings or symbols.

A vertical wedge (Y) stood for the number 1.

A corner wedge (◁) stood for the number 10.

A slightly larger vertical wedge (▽) stood for the number 60.

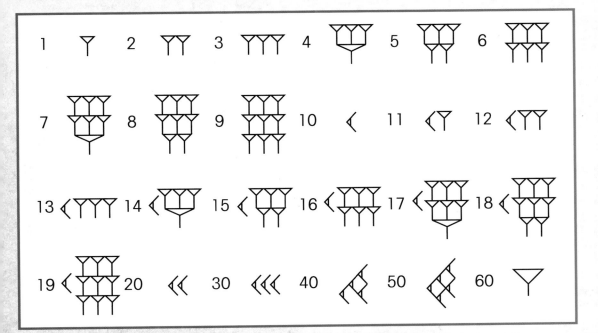

A farmer recorded the number of sheep he sold over 3 days in the table below. How many sheep did he sell in all?

day	1	2	3
sheep sold			

To solve this problem, first find out what numbers the cuneiform symbols represent.

This stands for the number 6.

This stands for the number 14.

This stands for the number 16.

The total number of sheep sold would be 6 + 14 + 16, or 36. The farmer sold 36 sheep in 3 days.

Can you write a word problem using the table? Use the problem we just solved as a model.

Early Calendars

Farming and agriculture played an important role in developing the civilizations of Mesopotamia. A more efficient system of measuring seasons and years became necessary. In addition, a tool was needed to help predict the coming of floodwaters from the Tigris and Euphrates rivers. To fill these needs, the Sumerians developed the first calendar.

This calendar was based on the phases of the moon. Each month, known as a lunar month, was equal to the number of days from 1 new moon to the next. Each year consisted of 12 lunar months. Since the lunar year was shorter than a solar year, the Sumerians added a "leap month" every 3 or 4 years in order to catch up with the sun. Today, we have a similar practice. We add 1 day to the end of February during years we call leap years.

In ancient times, years were named according to the ruler who reigned during that time. During Hammurabi's rule, the fifth year was called the "fifth year of Hammurabi's rule." This figure of Hammurabi kneeling to the gods was created around 1790 B.C., in the first year of Hammurabi's rule.

Leap years occur every 4 years. However, a year that is evenly divisible by 100 is not a leap year, unless the year is also evenly divisible by 400.

Given the years 1900, 1956, 1985, and 2000, can you tell which year is a leap year? To do this, divide each of the years by 4. If there is no remainder and the year fits the other rules above, the year is a leap year.

The year 1900 is evenly divisible by 4. It is also evenly divisible by 100, but not by 400. It is not a leap year.

The year 1956 is evenly divisible by 4. It is not evenly divisible by 100. It is a leap year.

The year 1985 is not evenly divisible by 4. It is not a leap year.

The year 2000 is evenly divisible by 4. It is also evenly divisible by 100 and 400. It is a leap year.

Was the year you were born a leap year?

Mesopotamian Mathematics

Just as the Sumerians needed to develop a written language, a number system, and a calendar, other Mesopotamian settlements needed mathematics to assist in agriculture and engineering as well. Later Mesopotamian peoples—like the Babylonians—adopted the Sumerian number system and used it to develop other forms of mathematics. There was a need for a system of weights and measures to help in the harvesting, storing, and division of foods. Better methods were needed for canal and **reservoir** construction and for dividing land among the people. Increasing trade required new practices for raising and collecting taxes. Many believe that the Babylonians used the Sumerian number system, which was based on the number 60, to form the basis for the 360-degree circle, 60-second minute, and 60-minute hour, all units of today's mathematics.

Some think the Sumerians may have studied the movement of stars—the home of their star gods—and divided the sky into 60 units.

Let's create a word problem that involves converting units of time. When we work with time, we may need to convert a unit to another unit. For instance, 120 seconds is equal to 2 minutes. Three hours is equal to 180 minutes. Look at the following problem:

Suppose that a Babylonian city-state required each farmer to devote 23,400 seconds to farming each day. How many hours would a farmer work each day?

To solve this problem, divide 23,400 seconds by 60 seconds to find the number of minutes.

$$
\begin{array}{r}
390 \text{ minutes} \\
60 \overline{)23,400} \\
-180 \\
\hline
540 \\
-540 \\
\hline
00
\end{array}
$$

There are 390 minutes in 23,400 seconds. Now divide 390 minutes by 60 minutes to find the number of hours.

$$
\begin{array}{r}
6.5 \text{ hours} \\
60 \overline{)390.0} \\
-360 \\
\hline
300 \\
-300 \\
\hline
0
\end{array}
$$

Each farmer would work 6.5 hours a day.

Now try to create your own word problem using different units of time.

The Babylonian number system differed from the earlier Sumerian number system. The similarities between the symbols for the number 1 and the number 60 (see chart on page 20) led to the 2 numbers eventually being represented by the same symbol. This led to the development of the Babylonian **positional principle** for numbers 60 and greater. To help explain this positional principle, let's take a closer look at our number system.

The number system that we use every day is based on the number 10 and is called the base 10 system, or decimal system. It is a positional, or place-value, system. The value of a number depends on its position. Each position represents a certain amount of tens in the number.

Place Value for Base 10				
ten thousands	thousands	hundreds	tens	ones
10^4	10^3	10^2	10^1	10^0
10 × 10 × 10 × 10	10 × 10 × 10	10 × 10	10	1
10,000	1,000	100	10	1

Let's take a look at the number five thousand two hundred thirty-six. Written as a numeral, this would be 5,236. In a place-value chart for base 10, this number would look like this:

ten thousands	thousands	hundreds	tens	ones
10,000	1,000	100	10	1
	5	2	3	6

$$5,236 = 5(\text{thousands}) + 2(\text{hundreds}) + 3(\text{tens}) + 6(\text{ones})$$
$$= 5(1,000) + 2(100) + 3(10) + 6(1)$$
$$= 5,000 + 200 + 30 + 6$$
$$= 5,236$$

Like base 10, the Babylonian base 60 system was a positional, or place-value, system. However, in base 60, each position represents a certain amount of sixties in the number. Compare the chart below to the base 10 chart on the opposite page.

Place Value for Base 60			
60^3	60^2	60^1	60^0
60 x 60 x 60	60 x 60	60	1
216,000	3,600	60	1

Suppose you read a Babylonian tax record which told of a certain number of sheep given by a farmer to a city-state government. You read the base 60 number as 2,14. What would be the equivalent of that number in base 10?

To solve this problem, use a chart to help you understand the value of the position of each number.

60^3	60^2	60^1	60^0
216,000	3,600	60	1
		2	14

Create an equation and solve.

$$2,14 = 2(\text{sixties}) + 14(\text{ones})$$
$$= 2(60) + 14(1)$$
$$= 120 + 14$$
$$= 134$$

Therefore, 2,14 in base 60 is equivalent to 134 in base 10.

Most of what we know about Mesopotamian mathematics comes from the Babylonian period around 1800 B.C. The Babylonians believed in creating and solving word problems. The focus on how best to solve a problem was characteristic of Babylonian studies. Many ancient Babylonian texts have related groups of problems that all have the same answer. This made computations easy yet placed great emphasis on the way the problem was solved.

Most of the tablets and texts from this time period are loaded with word problems about measurement. The Babylonians used geometrical constructions when building cities, walls, and ziggurats. Therefore, most of the geometric problems dealt with lengths, widths, diagonals, and volumes. Babylonian mathematics had no measurements for angles, which developed at a later time in history.

Let's take a look at a problem that Mesopotamian students may have solved. We will use base 10 for our calculations.

Some Babylonian math problems had to do with finding canal lengths, weights of stones, lengths of reeds, areas of fields, and numbers of bricks used in building. This tablet shows a problem in cuneiform script as well as a diagram.

The foundation for a ziggurat measures 297 feet long, 297 feet wide, and 3.3 feet tall. What is the volume of the foundation?

Volume is equal to length times width times height. Use the formula V = lwh to solve the problem.

$V = 297$ feet x 297 feet x 3.3 feet

```
      297
    x 297
    2 079
   26 73
  +59 4
   88,209
```

```
      88,209
    x     3.3
    26 462 7
  +264 627
   291,089.7
```

The volume of the foundation is 291,089.7 cubic feet.

Can you create a word problem using the volume formula? All you need is 3 of the following 4 measurements: volume, length, width, and height.

Contributions of Mesopotamia

Just as the first civilization grew from the fertile soil of the Tigris and Euphrates river valley, mathematics in Mesopotamia grew out of the necessity of keeping records of crops. By the Old Babylonian Empire of Hammurabi, mathematics had become more developed as civilization became more complicated. Archaeologists have recovered thousands of mathematical and economic tablets in the past century that have helped us to understand the progress that was made over thousands of years.

Many of the contributions in mathematics given to us by the peoples of Mesopotamia are still evident. Our system of keeping time, our calendar, and the origins of our place-value system of math are all rooted in this ancient period. After learning about the origins of civilization, it is easy to understand the importance of math in improving modern civilization as well. The ancient practice of solving problems is as necessary for us today as it was for the Mesopotamian peoples of ancient times.

Glossary

archaeological (ahr-kee-uh-LAH-jih-kuhl) Relating to the study of material remains of past human societies.

Asia Minor (AY-zhuh MY-nuhr) A peninsula in western Asia that is bounded on the north by the Black Sea, on the south by the Mediterranean Sea, and on the west by the Aegean Sea.

domesticate (duh-MEHS-tih-kayt) To tame an animal.

flax (FLAKS) A plant whose seeds can be used for food and oil and whose fiber can be spun to make cloth.

irrigation (ihr-uh-GAY-shun) Supplying water to fields by ditches, canals, or other man-made means.

legacy (LEH-guh-see) Something transmitted to those who come later.

positional principle (puh-ZIH-shuh-nuhl PRIHN-sih-puhl) A number system in which the value of a digit depends on its position in a number; a place-value system.

reservoir (REH-zuh-vwahr) A man-made lake where water is collected and stored.

theocracy (thee-AH-kruh-see) A state ruled by religious laws.

ziggurat (ZIH-guh-raht) An ancient temple shaped like a step pyramid.

Index